Tell it like it is

Poems by Pam Judge

Published by New Generation Publishing in 2021

First Edition

ISBN 978-1-80031396-5

www.newgeneration-publishing.com

Contents

Fine words don't butter no parsnips

She likes her parsnips raw, unbuttered,
crunchy, sweet, bits in her teeth,
plain food for a plain person.

Her poems are plain too,
a menu of metaphors
is not for her.

She prefers crudities to obscurities,
the crisp coolness of uncomplicated verse
that says what it means without accompaniment.

Canterbury Tale
(1942)

A three year old child sits
easy on the floor buttressed
by her mother's legs.
They are listening to hell.

The child doesn't know
Canterbury, York and Exeter
are the quarry culled
from Baedeker
in revenge for Lubeck.
50,000 houses disappear.
The high street is flattened.

Churchill knew but didn't tell.

The child knows
daddy's camp is near;
daddy's guard dog looking
at her through the wire
has shiny eyes and silky fur.

1939-1945

Electric woman
Fire raiser bent
on self-destruction.

One iron dangling
from an overhead flex
straight through the ironing-board.
One pan blazing,
mother and child hiding behind
the meat-safe,
with a broom
poking at gas-taps.
One electrocution,
you blue with volts
running upstairs to the flat above.
One jumper burning
(you were warming yourself at the gas-stove)
the wool was thick,
that and my screams
saved you.

These were your sorties
your raids
your invasions
when the men were at war.

It is now 2006,

Your ashes are waiting
in a spare bedroom.
It is the conclusion
a part of you had intended.

The poet addresses the vicar who stole her books

You were a good man, I have no doubt,
yet you 'stole' my books using the hook
of moral blackmail in your cold, old church.

I was an easy target for 'the poor of Rotherhithe':
the sort who stayed for the full three hours it took
for the Christ to die on his lonely cross.
I was easily impressed by holiness and sacrifice,
so I sacrificed:
        Little Women, hard backed in green
        Little Jenny Wren, her picture on the cover
        Little Jack Frost, wreathed in icicles and stars
        and Thumbelina, left alone on her lily-pad
        by the swallow impatient for the sun
but worst of all
        I handed over to your Christmas appeals
        Clark Gable, Constance Bennett, Jean Harlow,
        Ronald Coleman, Greta Garbo, Errol Flynn,
        sleekly glamorous in black and white in my
        mother's film annuals.

I am still cross, more than sixty years on, scouring,
  occasionally,
secondhand book shops hoping for a not too costly
  reunion.

She wears her clothes as if they were thrown upon her with a pitchfork

Jonathan Swift

Guilty

I cannot bear to let coats go and so
they last for years and years until
quietly, without any fuss, they fall
apart or end up in the garage as
garden coats fastened with paper-
clips or in the shed wrapping tools
and clothing bicycles. I respect my
coats, I feel emotional about them,
my gratitude is immense. They
state my point of view and say
'there, there, you are what you are
there's nowt you can do about it so
relax baby, be yourself and bugger
appearances.' Pitchfork indeed!

The Nail

She thought it was about DIY
the reason why, blow after blow
she hammered the nail spurned
by the wall, blow after blow, not
a trickle of dusty acceptance

not so much as a trickle of dust
as she hammered, hammered
and swore, would not give up,
knew she should have a masonry
pin, but the nail, nail, nail, would
not go into thc wall, wall, wall,
needing a drill, drill, drill, till
the nail gave way and snapped.

She thought it was about DIY
the reason she hammered
and hammered, blow after blow
on the head of the nail.

Handyman

I have to hand it to you,
living hand to mouth
you hand yourself
my computer, my telephone, my postcode
one of the beds, (not mine)
my washing machine, my larder, my space,
etcetera etcetera.

You want to be hand-in-glove
with me as long as it suits you
then you let go of my hand to fly,
no hand baggage weighing you
down with memories to tie your
hands, for you the secondhand
is always new.

I examine my hands, find them
empty; you can go, dear, as far
and free as you want to be,
my handout, a gift to you from me.

Poetic Measures

The poetry of an ordered cupboard:
a thrifty household economy

The poetry of cleared drains:
free flowing and sweet smelling

The poetry of washing on a line:
fabric filled with fresh air and sunlight

The poetry of a tidied house:
the necessary litter sorted

The poetry of housework:
virtues of a good vacuum

without clean cupboards: rats
without good drains: plague
without washing-lines: global warming
without a tidy house: disordered lives
without housework: no place like home
without a coffee after: no poetry.

Early Swim

Cold inundation
Stretch – split
Reach
Fling forward
Breathe
Find the rhythm

Lap and bubble
Pull and coil
Turn
Submerge
Rise

Legs
Thrash the water
Send up chlorine droplets

Archimedes screw
Vertebrae
Expand – contract
Loosen

On your back
Arms flailing
Old paddle steamer
Creaking along the Nile

Side-stroke
Head cushioned in water
Curling as on a pillow

Slap – Slap – Slap
Mind slows
Aqua- hypnosis
Perception piscine

Echoes on skin
Watery meditation

Friction

The return of tarmac was a cause for celebration;
motorists may have enjoyed dicing with ice
but not for ever, and we were dreaming of spring,
a green new year, snowdrops poking hope
through iron earth, each day palely, patiently
inching towards a wintery light of fitful gleams.

There is an ur-memory in her head
of unconsciousness that surfaces
when she swims, careful of sides
and ends, she shrinks from contact
that was made, not made with ice.

She relishes friction, its steady grip
which holds her fast, to-and-fro
grounded; stopped from slipping
between the lines of her life.

Ambush

spring is driving
my mind
road sense is unreliable

blossom plots
at worst
my demise
or someone-else's
at best disfigurement
of paintwork

lilac leaps at mc
laburnum lariats
try to lasso me
chestnut catkins
pierce my gaze
may hedgerows
seduce me

it's a conspiracy

Of fast lanes and frog tunnels

we have our purposes
the frogs and I
for the frogs
there is a tunnel
purpose-built
under the footpath
leading to the
customary ditch
where they
cast their spawn
my way is set
in the fast lane
of the M6 where
I am driven
beyond the limit
to see my own
little wrigglers
and so instinct
drives us on
elderly ladies
and frogs sharing
in regeneration
keeping the world
going round

Blackbird lane

Trodden many years of necessity
deep grooved between the fields,
comforting feet with years of leaves
pressed into a composted carpet,
a talking highway, we hear its story.

Travelers have passed and repassed
in to and fro commerce, bushes
are thick with memories and ghosts.
The lane is timeless, protected for us
by ancient liberties enshrined in law.

Blackbird Lane sings to us as we walk,
a song hundreds of years old. We too
shall pass, our lives bounded by time,
but, out of time, in this lane, we sense
a suspension that seems like eternity.

Theatre Critic

My pineal gland has an eye for bad plays
Writes its reviews in melatonin
Protects me from boredom through bio-rhythm
And sends me to sleep in the first act.

To those of you who might be tempted to say
That age induces my drowsiness
I would say ‘perhaps’
But then I would ask you why it is

That on certain nights I take my seat
Mind still cluttered with the day’s events
The curtain lifts, the play begins
And sends the litter blowing from my brain.

A War Grave is opened by the UN

I see them on TV
working conscientiously
to sort the bodies,
it's a jigsaw
this man's boot
under that man's neck,
fingers, in another man's
jaw, are prized gently away.

In a laboratory
a tattoo is scraped clean
with a nylon scourer,
carefully in case the skin
comes off with the mud.
A photograph is taken.
Bones are washed by hands
in pink kitchen gloves.

A watch, still going, is teased
from a papery wrist, tweezers
poke for the bullet buried
in the flesh still remaining.
It was revealed by X-ray
'the sort that used to be
in shoe shops' says an elderly
investigator smoking a pipe.

Body parts in black plastic bags
await identification through
the clothes piled on top,
some colours still visible.
An ambulance driver's pay
is still in his wallet, notes
unsullied, neatly folded,
survivors in the farmer's field.

Balkan Wars 1991.2001

The Map that came to Life

Ronald Lampitt 1948

Written to re-introduce children to the countryside after WW2

John and Joanna are off to Dumbleford
in knee-high socks and lace-up shoes.
Jo Jo the dog is bounding between them.
They put him on a lead where there are sheep.

On Dingle's farm they learn that crows
are not rooks, that steel pylons feed
the National Grid, cosy toes in towns
on wintcr nights. Thc clms bcing felled
will make fine farm buildings; scouts must
pitch tents away from trees and the damp.

Goodness how much they have learnt, and
scarcely started. Joanna needs a hand to pull
up the hill, but John doesn't mind, he's a boy.

What's this? They've come to the edge of - -
Oh dear, they've fallen right off into - -
a Ted Hughes poem. What's that hot stink?
What is the hawk doing with that bird's head?
Why is the lamb such a funny shape?
Why are those fish eating each other?
What is that gash in its throat?

What is that screaming? Why is it so cold?

Joanna begins to cry, she wants
to go home to muffins and tea
and mummy consoling. John
is bewildered, this is not in the script.
What shall they do? Do shut
Up Joanna! Trust a girl to start blubbing!

Help them Mr Lampitt, for they are lost.

The Lady's Reply

Had we but world enough and time
This coyness, lady, were no crime.

Your poetry is exquisite, your proposal enticing.
Your arguments are really quite enlightening but,
My dear, your proposition can only be called deceitful.
You propose sexual intercourse as sport
From my point of view this has import
Not applicable to you

I'm talking of conception: consider, if you will,
My weight gains, labour pains, the complications:
Breech births still births, fistulas, fevers, and flings-
Yours not mine, you wouldn't fancy me fat.
Episiotomies, prolapses, mastitis and post-natal
Blues. To sum up, the Church has it right:
'the great pain and peril of childbirth'. In the
'Churching of Women' additionally
A phrase states quite unconditionally, that
'Happy is the man that has his quiver full'
Of children, they mean, and I wonder, would
Your quill provide for us all, or would you move on?

I feel honoured that you have celebrated my beauty
In such an enduring fashion, and believe me when I say
That I am not without passion, but I must decline
Your offer, and I beg your pardon for saying, 'Go,
Plant your 'vegetable love' in someone else's garden.

Toulouse and Me

I am conducting a love affair
with Henri de Toulouse Lautrec
which has its difficulties since
he died, mad, at thirty five
and a long time ago.
I wouldn't have liked him,
what with the company he kept
and dives he frequented, but, oh,
all his love and pity paints
his way into my disapproving heart.

On the patio

Bright sunshine, a moving black dot rushes the print
of my Guardian page, scurries to the next paragraph,
balances along the edge of the paper, scuttles
down the reverse, disappears from view. Such elan!
My afternoon torpor is reproached. I mow the lawn.

Broil

A Sunday of fretfulness has fashioned me
out of sorts. Mardy, Fremmer and Freak
are soliciting my attention in a matter of divorce.

There has been a breakdown, a narky fratch
between Euphoria Lief and Megrim Moper;
I am cited by both parties as co-respondent

on the grounds of my widdershin tendencies
my feckless crack, my clarty thoughts, and
the mysterious hocus-pocus of my poetry.

What to say in my defence? Nowt or owt?
Listen, I am not faffing about, I'm mithered,
So either put up or shut up, or get out.

We can fettle our ways with give and take
or you can flit. I will continue my humdrum
days in content cack-handed cussedness.

Flummery

There's a civil war between my gut and me:
I should like to be a Cavalier, feasting on cream
and caviar, strong-tasting venison, pheasant,
oysters and syllabub slipping down, chased
by the best champagne and a lingering liqueur.
But there's a stovepipe hat in my heart and
a fear of flummery in my stern stomach
that will not tolerate such fancies, so, it's
the lettuce leaf for me, the root vegetable,
skimmed milk and Lurpak Light instead
of butter. My beleaguered Cavalier salivates
at the thought of a rare rump steak soaked
in red wine, dressed with garlic butter,
sometimes sneaked in when the Puritan
is asleep or looking the other way. But
it doesn't take much for hostilities to be
resumed, Regicide attempted, the whole
system flummoxed until digestion is pacified,
the body's Commonwealth restored

Memory

Hippocampus, ancient primal
mirror-image in the brain,
double sea-horses in the head:
necessary, but giving ground
to cortex in the human species.

The guardian of memory, it is
the first to fail in age when
words desert, sense of self
is eroded, space is dislocated,
no memories can be stored.

Woman mislays the middle,
unhappy years of her life;
mute, except for early rhymes
and songs; man exiled from
his life, everywhere but in
the present, his sea-horses
drowning in agitated unknowing.

Now record-keeping rides on the body:
scars on his hands, timbre of his voice,
his smiles, his touch, his smell,
all that remains to tell his story.

Home

slippers
shoes
good brown leather lace-ups

sandals
shoes
fabric shoes from the dispensary

shoes
shoes
some of them were yours

glasses
framed
without frames

on
off
lost

on
off
lost

teeth
in
out

in
out

lost
lost

room
is it mine?

where is my room?

The Visit

1

There is a sweetness in it,
two old people dozing after lunch
father and daughter in front of a blazing fire,
all the Patience Strong poems you've ever read
rolled up into one calm togetherness.
Winter sun gleams through the windows,
daffodils pushing up in the winter garden.

2

I have taken you back to the Home
from whence mum escaped quietly
one night, so quietly, quietly,
her little mouth open as if to say
'What's all the fuss? No need to get excited,
pretend I'm just asleep as you slip my rings
off my fingers. I did love you once
but it doesn't matter now'

3

You glance at the frame by your bed
where the photo proclaims that
a room was hers, here, when she cared
enough to stay alive in it.
You say nothing.
I leave you,
return to unquiet death on the TV.

Landslip

The landscape is sliding out
of a childhood turning indoors
out of the wind and rain, out
of wild places, away from
adder and ash, buttercup,
conker, kingfisher, newt,
otter and ivy, and into bullet
point, blog, broadband,
Instagram, Tik Tok, computer games.

'For blackberry, read Blackberry'

Common and heath no longer
for children to roam together-
what else are phones for – no
more stinging nettles and bracken
burns, no more burrs on your
socks, creeping grass climbing
your sleeves as you hurry home
dirty, knees streaked with blood.

Attachment has a new meaning.

Note: 2015 OUP has admitted eliminating
words from its Junior Dictionary
that it no longer considers so relevant to a
modern-day childhood.

Alice in Wonderland

Password:Trojan Horse Back Door Darkbot.H

She is inside her Trojan Horse, eyes staring
into the darkness, ears pinned to the walls
listening for the magic words she does not
understand. She hears the chanting, muttering,
whispering voices of the multiverse:

A pion consists of an up and an anti-down quark yield,
a particle of only 139.6Me V of mass energy, while
in the rho vector meson, the same combination of quarks
has a mass of 770Me V

the voices continue:

they have guessed she is listening and simplify,

Your history begins with Bangs and Bounces, all big
and possibly continuous; Crunches too may finish
the stew of mesons and baryons, bosons, pions and hadrons

the whispers grow faint

and morons
this last, a scientific term of abuse when scientific
minds
bend under the weight of gravity

the voices recover

for you must know that space is expanding, possibly without limit,
until without any mass whatever the earth will be vaporized
OR, maybe, the universe will contract into a density called the Big Crunch
OR turned into ice in the Big Freeze
OR Dark Energy, of which there is a lot, will cause atoms to shatter

At this point she stops listening, the air has grown foetid, her head aches,
the walls are closing in, she cannot breathe. She has to break out into
Wonderland, to spy, in disguises, both large and small, as she tries to
EAT ME and DRINK ME into the multiverse.

Author's note – you shouldn't have read this poem if you are an astrophysicist.

The Sniff

The sisters' sniff
delicate
in petal noses
is ladylike
identical

Patricia
pats her nose
set in
pink parchment cheeks
under clear blue eyes

So familiar
a sniff can survive
oceans and years apart
a perfect signature
of sisterhood

Dead Tree

You're not fooling me, this is not autumn,
leaves should conceal those starkly beautiful,
black branches: you are masquerading, my
dear, I know you for what you are: dead.

It is high, green-crowded summer: too
much ripeness anticipates rot, stifles
breathing. Stripped bone, you stand
in your grave, mute witness and host.

Yesterday, upon the stair

I met a (woman) who wasn't there
Apologies to William Hughes Mearns

We are the absent women displaced
from your stories. Lady Bertram's maid,
Mrs Dalloway's char, Daisy's neglected
daughter, Lady Deadlock's skivvy.

Our lives are untold but we are there
unsettling the narrative if you care
to consider the shadows: labours
taken for granted, affections denied,
icy sheets, aching limbs on back stairs.

You may wish we would go away but
we are obstinate, we will make you look
at us between the lines of your book,
remember us, the ones not written.

Reading the Walls

Also SARAH
Wife of the above

who died twelve years before he did,
John, who was not 'Also' and in larger
letters too.

ANNA
Relict of William Plumbe

Fared better than her husband, still alive
'relict' for thirty lone, long years to1875.

On a tablet in the church a sub-heading records

Mrs Mary Barford
Daughter of the Above

Three times married Lady Periam reclines in marble.
She is not recorded as wife, relict, daughter, of anyone.
Husbands, listed below her name, left her able to give
money to an Oxford College, endowing scholarships,
schooling for poor, bright boys of the parish.
Her epitaph is written in Latin, lists virtues all her own.

'It's my party - - -

It went wrong from the start:
the children did not do as they
were told. History has blamed
her. I don't entirely, the odds
were stacked, beastly, base,
insinuating, my licensed foe.
He first thought of the fig leaves,
she did the sewing, being practical;
each was complicit.

Since then, I have been in a sulk
quite frankly, firstly the Flood,
earthquake, wind and fire for
a fillip now and then when I am
in a mood.

Things are not improving:
it's difficult to shake off a mood.
The tears keep falling in spite
of myself; I can't help it if
the Maldives disappear, too
much partying there anyway;
if I'm not enjoying myself, I
don't see why anyone else should.
It's my world and I'll cry if I want to.

Missing

I miss Him, the Big Cheese, the One
who lit the sun and ordered the stars,
guaranteed the future of my immortal
soul, numbered the hairs on my head,
who was my friend.

Now, the universe is empty
of everything except the Wonder:
scientists are now the new High priests
voicing an oracle which only they
can try to interpret.

We are grown-ups now; orphaned,
bewildered, blundering towards death,
determined to go out in style, divas,
belting out the final aria, consumptive
but insisting on being heard.

Liking it Hot

You are a witness to crimes you didn't commit,
fleeing from the guilt of it, weighed down,
wobbling on heels that are too high for you,
pursing lips and wiggling hips as you rush
to catch the train that you hope will whisk you
away from trouble, but trouble has boarded
the train with you, all the way.

And trouble is hot: a ukulele blonde barges into
your life sucking the fuzzy end of the lollipop which
she offers to you in spite of Sweet Sue. You duck
and you dive, in and out of trouble's coils, faster
and faster until you don't know who you are
and you are dancing the fandango, a rose between
your teeth, merrily mismatched, but wearing a smile
like the smile on the face of the tiger.

Image

She is a violent woman, she does not weep,
she acts. She has always been like this:
Judith, Jezebel, Deborah, Delilah,
and Jael
with her hammer and nail,

but she became a victim of Art.

written, painted, confined to an image
he has of her:
languishing in her moated grange;
cradling her baby in her arms;
titillating in celluloid,
turning from her window,
Marianna, Mary, Marilyn,
the Lady of Shalott.

The Long View

To be ripe like Lawrence’s apples:
scented, stored in the attic,
not shriveled but glowing,
no bad apples oozing with bile.
The window open to the long view.

Forty Trillion Pleasure Song

We are multitudes in your maturity, at home
in every part of you, curiously intimate,
sporting in your eyebrows, swimming in
your gut. We colonise you in the birth canal
and we decompose you when you die. We
love you and you owe us your long lives.
Your navel is our pleasure park. We play
at mutations, swapping our cells to outwit you
at every turn; technically, some of us being
arachnids, we laugh at your fear of spiders.

Our years are measured in billions; we are deep
in the rocks and up to the highest blue. We are
the imperium surfing the universe: you can find
us on asteroids and moons seeding your existence.
You do not yet know us.

Covid 19

We leap, floating on droplets, myrmidons
obeying a single impulse: to replicate.
We are fast. You are close in your alliances,
we close with your tissues and soon we are
everywhere. Subverters of your codes, we
infiltrate, become your essence; you do not
know our beginning or your end

My sister

Goes to sleep in the theatre,
gazes at me in wonderment
when I am in floods of tears
for Madam Butterfly.
She adores the Stones and
inexplicably, Star Trek.

She has green fingers,
is a cordon-bleu cook;
has an unerring eye
for the truth of things.

Along with bananas and ice-cream
I acquired a baby sister post-war,
perhaps a bit too late for a playmate
but I wouldn't be without her.

The Whirligig of Time

The children are talking to me,
my voice, my words, from twenty
years ago: good sense then, good
sense now, same result, ‘No’.

Thus advice! Cassandras all of us,
generation to generation,
with this reservation: we believe
and are believed but we don’t
want to be reminded-not yet!

Convalescence

First fitness walk after a hip replacement

I am walking down an uneven field.
Four horses of the almost Apocalypse
gallop at speed towards me. Death
seated on the first pale horse leading
the charge.
What to do?
Look him sternly in the face,
stand stock still.
It's not working.
Summon teacher tones, 'No No No'
stick raised horizontal as shown on TV.

Pale horse is puzzled, was he expecting
apples? He swerves but not so chestnut
who continues straight at me, War shining
in his eyes. Am I to be mown down by Beauty?
I step aside, horse slows past, takes frustration
out on first horse.
I walk on.

When I look back all four horses
are grazing peacefully, butter
wouldn't melt

Big Toe

Big toe complains:
'I am not taken seriously enough'
even on Wikipedia.

'this article needs restructuring
qualifying, additional citing'

Big Toe asserts his importance:
I keep you upright, balanced,
not a pretty sight but necessary
to vertical ascendancy.

Big Toe is depressed
too much pressure:
shoes too tight, heels too high,
soles too thin,
pressure, pressure, pressure.

Big Toe recites his woes:
hallux valgus,
blisters,
fungus,
ingrowing toenail,
gout.

Big toe delivers a warning:
remember me in the pride of your youth,
treat me disdainfully and I will pay you back
painfully.

Scarecrow Song

We are scarecrows now, hollowing
gently out of ourselves, we follow
a well-trodden path through the woods
into the fallow. An old familiar song
echoes in the memory, diminishing chords
hurry us towards the Coda.

Emptying disturbance and flummery
we become clear-sighted, simplified.
Past-life hangs round us as weather-
ravaged clothes on scarecrow crosses,
colours not quite faded but raggedy.
We smile as winter winds sound coldly.

We will become increasingly see through
but our staves will define and hold us.

Queen of Tact

(the DAFT award for teachers)

It’s official!
I’m queen of tact
I have a certificate to prove it
from the Sixth Form.

My family
had better take note
(it hangs on the wall in a spare bedroom)
and believe it
otherwise
the cynical little sods
won’t get any supper.

So there!

Losing

Losing your way in Cumbria is easy
I do it beautifully, following the sun
East or West shining
finding
red squirrels in Eden
wild horses on Caldbeck
buzzards high-flying Blencathra
rooks fretting the bare branches
of winter trees
a puff of rainbow driven
across slopes at Cross Fell.

I travel with
the Maid of Buttermere
the Quakers of Mosedale
Ruskin, declining over Coniston
Coleridge, night-hiking from St Bees
Dorothy, noting seasons around Rydale.

Losing your way in Cumbria is easy
I do it beautifully,
roads taken justify themselves
without metaphor or allegory,
leading to poetry.

Corona Spring

Horse immobile stands
patient in spring sunshine, all
mute resignation

Daffodils breeze-dance,
falsely-fleeting, harbingers
of mortality

Tulips in royal
colours challenge cold spring winds,
display bravura

Woodpecker, boldly
tapping at the tree, does not
mind an audience

Heron, all alert,
watches water unblinking
for unwary fish

Walkers smile, good dogs
snuffle, frozen earth gives firm
purchase; it's quiet!

Moon

‘th’ inconstant moon,
That monthly changes’

They call you
shape shifter
water splitter
mind skitter
listless satellite
inconstant moon

I call you
spirit lifter
soul searcher
measurer
harvester
constant moon

Her
horns and crown are ancient,
immaculate queen of heaven, she
rides you crescent, ascending
from the sea; Astarte, Mary,
her names are many; she measures
women against her perfections.

You
feed fantasies of June light and roses,
bear blame for mooncalves and period
pains. Lunatics are your creation and
harvest failures. Your magic dusts
the night air with moondrops.
Never fickle, a constant companion
to earth, whose moonstruck dreamers
touch tenderly your light, your dark .

spirit splitter
soul shifter
mind searcher
measurer
harvester
constant moon

Of bees, borzois and buses

People are, at present, mostly virtual,
not so the bees or the three borzois
I met at the park before one of them
gathered his haunches, unleashed
his spine into an explosion of speed
to join other joyful dogs in a merry-
go-round of chase and greet, lady
in jodhpurs cheerfully explaining that
they make excellent pets for folk who
like hoovering.

Furry bumble-bees enjoy
my not so tidy garden with one tall weed
that sends them into ecstasies of bumbling
all summer long. Soon my Sweet Williams
will nurse honey bees into winter lockdown.

Empty buses trundle past my house faithful
to the timetable and the drivers' pockets.
We wait and contemplate the bees; we walk
our ways into an uncertain winter with our
dogs; one day we will catch a bus again.

www.ingramcontent.com/pod-product-compliance
Ingram Content Group UK Ltd.
Pitfield, Milton Keynes, MK11 3LW, UK
UKHW042000190726
13854UKWH00005B/2092

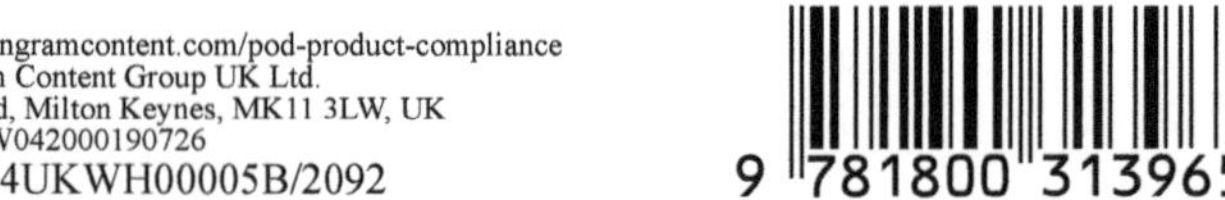

9 781800 313965